MISSIONS
IN THE
IMAGE OF GOD

AN EIGHT DAY BIBLE STUDY ON MISSIONS

Lynndon (Lynn) L. Thomas

The publisher of this book is,

The Ministry Council of the Cumberland Presbyterian Church

This edition was published for Lynndon L. Thomas, and the publisher is responsible for this edition's distribution. For information about permission to reproduce this edition (First Edition) of the book, contact:

Publications Manager,
Communications Ministry Team,
Cumberland Presbyterian Center,
8207 Traditional Place
Cordova (Memphis), Tennessee, 38016-7414.

The cover picture is of the suspension bridge in the Hadano Tokawa municipal park, Sagami, Japan.

All residuals from the sale of this First Edition are for the benefit of the Missions Ministry Team.

ISBN: 978-1-945929-31-1

Missions, In the Image of God

AN EIGHT DAY BIBLE STUDY ON MISSIONS

And Jesus came and said to them, "All authority in heaven and on earth has been given to me. Go therefore and make disciples of all nations, baptizing them in the name of the Father and of the Son and of the Holy Spirit, teaching them to observe all that I have commanded you. And behold, I am with you always, to the end of the age.
Matthew 28:18-20 (ESV)

The cover of this book shows a person walking over a bridge. Missions and missionaries are represented by this picture in that they cross cultural bridges to share the gospel of Jesus Christ. This Bible study will help you better understand the ministry of missions and the work of missionaries.

The Design of the Bible Study: This Bible study combines scriptures with concepts related to missions from mission leaders. By using scriptures, mission concepts, and church history, this study presents how the church should understand and do missions. The goal of this Bible study is to present a biblical perspective on missions that reflects God's image. This mission lesson is for those who are or who want to be students of missions. The study helps explain the work of missionaries and the importance of missions to the church. This study is unique, in contrast to other studies about missions, because it explains missions from a relational perspective. Mission provides a way for Christians to connect with other Christians and experience a global family. Missions has the ability to transform lives, not only on the mission field but also the life of the missionary and his or her sending church.

The Bible Study's Audience: This Bible study is intended for use in a Sunday School class, church sessions/boards, a Bible study group, or as a devotional. Each lesson ("day") in the Bible study is set up as a thirty to a forty-five-minute lesson. The lessons are arranged in mission topics. It is best to think of this Bible study as a class on missions. The study for the "day" could be conducted as a group Bible study that meets on a specific day or an individual study where the person does a study/devotional about missions.

How to Use the Study: Group Bible Study - It is best that this Bible study has a group leader to lead the lesson. This person can be the same each lesson, or the Bible study leader can rotate to different people. When the group meets, they can:

1. Start the lesson with prayer.
2. The group can use one of these two approaches:
    a. The group can study the lesson before they meet, and the leader of the group can conduct a review of the material and lead the group in discussions.

OR

    b. The leader can read the lesson aloud or ask each person to read parts of the lesson aloud, stopping for times of discussion.
3. Read the scriptures found in each lesson. The group's participants will need a Bible, as the verses are not written in the lessons. The fact the participants have their own Bibles means the group may have different translations, which is good. The group will read the verses and may compare different versions.
4. In the lesson you will see discussion questions. The discussion questions correspond to that part of the study where you see the question.
5. There are different ways to interact with the lesson. You will see "THINK" sections, which provide illustrations about the points being made in the lesson. The "THINK" sections often contain questions to discuss. There are also "ACTION" and "REFLECTION" ideas that will help you interact with the material.
6. At the end of each lesson, there is an announcement, "Looking Ahead," about what the next lesson will cover. At the close of each lesson is a reflection idea.

For those using this study for individual study or as a devotional – they may want to take notes. Obviously, there is no opportunity for group discussion around the questions, but it might be helpful to write down your thoughts as you read the questions and review the sections.

The Author: Lynndon (Lynn) Thomas is an ordained Cumberland Presbyterian (CP) minister. He and his family were missionaries in Colombia, South America for 11 years, from 1987 to 1998. Before going to Colombia, Lynn worked as a mission intern in various countries. After returning from Colombia to the USA in 1998, Lynn became the CP director of cross-cultural ministries USA, working on starting churches with immigrant populations in the USA. In 2011, he became the director of global missions for the CP Church, supervising missionaries and guiding CP ministries and church expansion.

Lynn is a graduate of Bethel University; he has a Master of Divinity from Memphis Theological Seminary, and a Doctor of Intercultural Studies from Fuller's School of Intercultural Studies. He is married to Nona, and they have four children.

For a more complete understanding of the concepts in this Bible study, consult the book, *Relational Missions, Concepts, Perspectives and Practices That Inform Global Missions*, by Lynn Thomas. This Bible study, in part, is based on that book.

Contents

Day One: The Call to Missions is Not a Call to Everything

Introduction: Missions is an essential part of the life of a church. Christians love to hear from missionaries and to learn about different mission fields. At the same time, there is a great deal of confusion about what missions is and who missionaries are. This lesson will help you appreciate your call by God to God's service, as well as understand the missionary call to missions.

<u>Scripture Review: Read Acts 13: 1-4</u>

In Acts 13:1, we read that Saul (Paul) and Barnabas attended the church of Antioch. This church was the result of the death, by martyrdom, of Stephan. Acts 8:1 and Acts 11:19 explain that Christians left Israel to escape death squads seeking to kill Christians. Interestingly, Saul was part of the death squads (Acts 8:1). Some of these people ended up in the Roman city of Antioch. There was a large Jewish population in Antioch, so the early Jewish Christians used relational networks and migrated to this city. Saul, after his conversion, and Barnabas, traveled to Antioch and became participants in this church. The Antioch Church was probably the first Christian church outside of Israel. Saul and Barnabas joined this group and remained with them for a year (Acts 11:25). In Acts 13: 2-3, the Bible explains that after a year, the Antioch Church laid hands on Saul and Barnabas and sent them to Cyprus and Galatia (Southern Turkey) as missionaries. Saul and Barnabas were the church's first official missionaries. Acts 13:4-23 explains what these missionaries did during their mission to this part of the world. They visited seven different cities on their journey. On their return back to Antioch, they stopped at several of these cities for a second visit to encourage the new believers. Saul and Barnabas returned to Antioch and gathered the church together to report on what had happened. Their big news was that the gospel message had been received by the Gentiles (Acts 14:27).

Discussion. What impact do you think sending Paul and Barnabas away had on the Antioch Church?

The mission professor Arthur Glasser notes that the Antioch Church leaders were fasting and praying. They were on their knees in humble worship. He believes they were asking God what their responsibility was as a church. They were seeking God's guidance. The Holy Spirit led them to do something they had never done before; they selected people from their church to leave. They commissioned these beloved church members to leave the country and travel to foreign lands. This is believed to be the first account of the church doing "foreign missions" (Winter et al. 2009, 150).

Action: Find a Bible with maps in the back and look for a map that says, "Paul's first missionary journey." If possible, look at that map in relation to a modern map (Google Maps) to see where Paul went.

THINK

As the director of missions, I was invited to give a mission presentation to a small group. It was an informal setting; those in attendance sat around a large table. After I shared about the different missionaries and the mission fields, I asked if there were any questions. One person seemed anxious and quickly blurted out, "I think we are all missionaries, and there is a great deal that needs to be done here in our community." I had heard this comment many times in many places. Missionaries and missions are an expensive endeavor.

I understand the concern some Christians have that too much emphasis is placed on missions. If missions is about what is best for the church, the concern about expense and benefit to the local church has merit. But what if missions is not about the church?

Mission Concept: Missionaries are Christians called by God and trained to cross over cultural barriers and share the gospel.

If missions is sharing the gospel and the growth of the local church, then the Acts 13 story produces a dilemma. Why would the church of Antioch, a small church in a large city where there were no other churches, sacrificially send two of their most capable evangelists to another country? Why would they sacrifice the human and material resources of their congregation, which had its own needs? The fact is, there was much outreach and ministry that needed to be done in Antioch.

When the statement is made that we are all missionaries, what should we call people who leave their country, acquire intercultural skills, and learn a new language and culture so that they can share the gospel? If we call everything the church does "missions," then what should we call the unique ministry of crossing cultures to share the gospel? Missions is not anything and everything Christians do.

It becomes apparent that the only title one can give a person with a call from God and specialized training to work outside their culture is, a "missionary." The specialized ministry of sending missionaries and the work they do in other countries is called "missions." Missionaries leave their church, community, and culture and go into a foreign world.

Discussion. Why is it important for the church to understand that missions is different than other ministries the local church does?

Evangelism, church planting, and helping others are often classified by some church leaders as "missions." Missions involves evangelism, church planting, and helping others, but mission involves a unique dynamic. These ministries are all done by crossing a cultural divide to do them. What if your pastor said, "we are all pastors." Most things our pastor does are things we should do. We should study God's word, visit the sick, teach about Christ to those who will hear us, and live holy lives. So, are we all pastors? Most realize that a pastor, as a missionary, is called to a vocation. They do many of the same things, but they do them in an entirely different context.

There are many organizations that send out missionaries, and some are more responsible than others. A responsible mission organization has expectations for their missionaries. A missionary should have a call from God to be a missionary. This "call" is much deeper than seeking an adventure or a tourist desire to travel and experience a new culture. The call to be a missionary means something happened in a person's life in which they felt God ask them to live on the mission field for a prolonged period. The consequence of the call is a desire to go. Usually, that enthusiasm is channeled into preparation and training to be a missionary. The missionary needs skills that can be used on the mission field.

Mission Concept: Missionaries are like pastors in that both are vocations with unique responsibilities that require special training and experience to be effective.

Denominations and responsible mission organizations require missionaries to have theological and cultural training. Some seminaries offer specialized training in missions. This area of training is called "missiology" or "intercultural studies." If a missionary is going to plant churches, they need experience as a pastor or evangelist. For example, Paul and Barnabas were not new inexperienced Christians. They were leaders in the church. Before a missionary goes to the mission field, he or she is expected to have an understanding of other cultures. The first thing a missionary will do is go to a language school, where he or she will study a new language for a year or two. Usually, it takes a new missionary about three years to acclimate to their new country. If a college student feels called to missions, it may take years of preparation before they go to the mission field.

THINK

A lady once approached me with tears in her eyes and said how amazing it was that I was a missionary. I was a missionary in South America and was visiting her church in the USA. She explained that she was impressed anyone would make such a sacrifice. I was confused. I was a missionary because I wanted to be one. Being a missionary was exciting and fulfilling. I loved it. I realized this dear lady thought I was suffering, I was not.

Why do people go to the mission field as missionaries?

Missions is a call, just like the call to be a pastor, church leader (elder, deacon), or Sunday school teacher. All the calls are of equal value. There is often the misconception that missionaries have a higher calling. That is not true; it is merely a call from God. All missionaries serve on the mission field because God called them, and they desire to be there. The same with pastors. A pastor serves as a pastor because their call from God produces a motivation to do the work of a pastor in a local church. Once called, they are trained. Are all Christians missionaries? Are all Christians pastors? Are all Christians elders/deacons?

Discussion. "A Calling" - What is your passion? What is the thing you like to do or would like to do for Christ as a Christian?

The concern most church leaders rightfully have are the needs of their local church. Countless hours are spent in meetings trying to arrange resources to meet local needs. The pragmatic response is, "why not take care of our own needs as a church; then we can worry about everyone else when we are better off." This perspective is a reasonable reaction to the request made to local churches to promote and support missions. Many churches take up a missionary offering, usually once a year. This offering is often a small percentage of the entire giving of that church. Is missions a ministry that the church supports after it supports the other important local ministries; or is missions something else? As we will see in this Bible study, missions is something else. In fact, you will discover that missions is not what the church does; it is what the church is.

Discussion. The local church must set priorities as to the use of resources; what should influence those priorities?

Missionaries are Christians that believe God called them to leave their country and go to another country to share the gospel. Missions is not like other ministries in the church. The church, acting as Christ's body on earth and as a representative of God, commissions people that it believes to be prepared and called by God's Spirit to the mission field. The sending church is then challenged to support missionaries and their mission sacrificially. Because God is the originator of missions, not the church, missionaries are called by God to go on God's mission. Missions is like a human body extending its hand to feed someone that is hungry. The hand is not detached from the body, it is an extension of the body. The entire body is called to feed the hungry, but the hand is the member that is sent because it has the skills to meet the need. However, when the church calls everything it does "missions," and everyone in the church a "missionary," the activity of missions and the vocation of the missionary is lost. We are not all hands. When there is no sacrifice, this indicates the church is on its own mission. The call does not stop with the missionary; the church too is called by God to missions. The church is sending itself, thus explaining the depth of the sacrifice the church is making.

Mission Concept: Missions imitates God by challenging the church to sacrifice itself for the gospel.

THINK

J.B. and A.D. Hail were brothers from Pennsylvania. They were both college-trained Cumberland Presbyterian ministers. They learned about Japan, and both brothers felt called to be missionaries. The Hail brothers approached their denomination's mission board and asked for their support, but there was no money. They then approached a group of Cumberland Presbyterian churches in the area where they lived and asked them for support. These churches raised enough to support one of the brothers. J.B. Hail and his wife sailed to Japan in 1877. A.D. Hail, who was also a pastor, went back to school to study medicine and wait for missionary support. A donor eventually paid his passage to Japan. These two brothers established churches in Japan that flourished. More missionaries soon joined them. The Hail brothers opened Japan as a mission field to the Cumberland Presbyterian Church. By the early 1900s, there were over 1,100 Japanese Christians affiliated with the Cumberland Presbyterian Church.

Both J.B. and A.D. Hail were intelligent and gifted church leaders. Many offerings and donations were made from churches in the USA to support their ministry in Japan.

If one of the Hail brothers were your pastor and had come to you for advice on going to Japan, what would you have told them?

God models the sending of missionaries by sending His Son. By sending God's Son, God sent God's self. As Jesus noted in the Gospel of John, "I and the father are one" (John 10:30 ESV). The activity of missions is to be in God's image. Missions is not cutting off the hand from the body. Missions is the entire body, through the hand, proclaiming the gospel to other cultures. God sent His Son and remained connected and committed to His Son while His Son was on God's mission. Missions is a sacrifice for the church, both by sending and by remaining connected. The church is in the image of God. Missions should be more than a small offering or an occasional time to pray for missionaries. Missions is the whole church in God's mission. The whole church is called, and therefore the church sends its own; it sends missionaries. They are not sent, disconnected, and forgotten; they are sent as an extension of Christ's Body.

Acts 13: 1-4 is a story about missions that is much larger than Paul and Barnabas. God called the Antioch Church to go on God's mission. And the Holy Spirit showed the church how. The church sent its hands, two of its best leaders as missionaries. These missionaries were a sacrifice for the sending church, and they were also sent as an extension of the Body of Christ.

Action: Think of people you know that are missionaries: talk about what you know of their ministry, what you know of the country where they work.

THINK

The word "mission" is derived from the Latin word "mitto," (misso) which means to send. The word is not found in the Bible. It was first used in 1544 by early Roman Catholic missionaries to explain the spread of the gospel. The word appeared in common use in the 1600s and was understood to mean "going out" on a journey to share the gospel. Prior to this term, and still found in many Christian writings, the word "apostolic" was used to describe going out to share the gospel (Ott and Netland 2006, xiv). David Bosch, a South African mission leader, notes that until the 16th Century, the term "missions" was exclusively related to the doctrine of the Trinity, that is, the Son and Holy Spirit being sent (2011, loc. 369).

Action: Find the Cumberland Presbyterian Confession of Faith and look at what it says about missions. The Confession uses the word "apostolic." This document was first written in the early 1800s and is representative of the language used in that era to talk about missions. This document can be found online using Google search (PDF file). By conducting a word search ("apostolic") in the document you will discover what this Protestant confession says about missions.

Looking ahead: In the next lesson, we will look at why the church does missions. By exploring church history, we will identify some of the problems the church has doing missions when the church has the wrong motivation for missions.

Reflection: Using a smartphone, tablet, or computer (with internet), find the YouTube video, "He is Worthy" by Andrew Peterson. Watch this music video and listen closely to the words of the song.

Day Two: The Church Expanding, What Could Be Wrong with That?

Introduction: There is no question in the mind of Christian leaders that there is a connection between missions and the church. This lesson will explain what that connection is. The hope is that once you understand the connection, you will be able to help your church understand its mission.

Scripture Review: Read Acts 15: 6-20

The early church of Acts quickly expanded from Jewish Christians to Gentiles. Gentiles increasingly accepted Jesus Christ, but they did not accept the Jewish customs and rituals of their Jewish Christian brothers and sisters. This reality created confusion among the church's leaders, all of which were Jews. The question was: can a Gentile become a Christian and not adopt Jewish customs and rituals? Up until this point in the church's history, all the Christians were Jews, and they had blended Christianity into their Jewish culture. The earliest church was only expanding into Jewish communities. First Century Jewish Christians followed Jewish dietary laws, accepted circumcision, and visited the Jerusalem Temple and synagogues.

Discussion. What Jewish customs received Gentile objections (Review Acts 15)? What aspects of Christianity should be the same for all Christians, and what aspects can be different because they represent a cultural preference?

The account in Acts 15: 1-29, tells how the Jewish leaders met in Jerusalem and discussed the issue of expansion and a problem it had created. The debate was intense (Acts 15: 7). Peter, Paul, and Barnabas were in attendance (Acts 15: 12-14). All three of them had seen Gentiles profess Christ and receive the Holy Spirit (Acts 15: 14-17). They told their stories. The Gentile Christians did not practice Jewish religious rituals. Jews had experience accepting Gentiles into Judaism as converts to the Jewish faith and its rituals, but Christian conversion was different. The Gentiles were reluctant to become Jews in order to be Christians. The council of church leaders concluded that Gentiles could become Christians (Acts 15: 19). The Jewish Christians said the Gentiles did not have to become Jews to be Christians. They wrote a letter that was to be shared among all Christian churches making the declaration that it was acceptable to be a Christian and not follow Jewish customs (Acts 15: 20-29). The reality of the decision was Jews and Gentiles would be part of the same faith family. The Christian Jews were expected to be a faith community with non-Jews. They all would be one in Christ.

The impact of this decision was monumental. Christianity was now a transcultural religion, which means it was above all cultures. The decision meant Christianity was not an expression or sect of Judaism. And most importantly, by allowing Christianity to flow into other nations and cultures, it became applicable to all peoples in the world, regardless of race, economic status, or culture. The church would be multi-cultural. The disciples were forced to determine what within Christianity was the gospel and what was just their Jewish culture. Every culture has to do the same reflection when sending missionaries from their culture. What parts of our values, beliefs, and norms are our cultural preferences, and what parts are truly the gospel? Because the church is transcultural, intercultural relationships force an answer.

Action: Think about your church's worship service. Make a list of the elements of the service that reflect your culture. Without these elements, your worship experience would feel foreign.

Mission Concept: The gospel always arrives on the mission field as a gift wrapped in a foreign culture. To receive the gift the wrapping paper has to be removed.

Let us look at church history to understand how the church struggled with intercultural relationships. The Roman Empire accepted Christianity 300 years after the birth of the church. Initially, Rome persecuted Christians, but by the reign of the emperor Constantine, Christianity was accepted and protected by Rome. The early church theologians, Augustine and Aquinas, realized that if the church and the state partnered, they could expand Christianity around the world (Bosch 2011, loc. 5705). Their vision was world evangelization through the church, with the help of the state. The hope was, with the help of the state and its resources and protection, the church could Christianize the world. Partnership with the state was a pragmatic approach to missions.

The church, for many centuries, was the Roman Catholic Church. There was only one church; the Catholic Church understood itself to be "The Church of Christ." This understanding propelled the church and state into the world, establishing Christian churches. Although the gospel message was proclaimed throughout the world, the motives for missions were mixed. On the one hand, there was a genuine desire that people be baptized in the name of Christ and join the church. On the other hand, the state was able to use the church to expand the state's power and dominance around the world. This approach of missions was far from the idea of the church sacrificially being sent as Christ's body to be one in Christ with all nations.

Discussion. What are converts joining when they are baptized? Is baptism membership into the local church, or is it something else?

THINK

The church must be careful and not entangle missions with secular powers that seek to use missions for its own motives. At the same time, missions must be protected from those within the church that seek to use missions as a way to advance other activities not related to missions.

In the late 1800s and early 1900s, mission endeavors within denominations used a separate "board" that conducted foreign mission work. Denominations did two things, "home" ministries and "foreign" missions. These two activities were usually under two separate legal governing boards. But by the middle of the 20th Century, the trend was to dissolve the mission board and place missions alongside the other ministries of the denomination. Although mission leaders often resisted this change, the numerous ministries of the denomination and their leaders thought that missions should not be a separate activity of the church. Missions was now under one board and consequently in direct competition for resources with other ministries of the denomination. As well, these other denominational ministries were increasingly calling what they did "missions." By the 1980s, many mission programs became focused on humanitarian assistance. Missions was sending help to those in need, not so much sending missionaries. This change resulted in an explosion of non-denominational mission organizations that focused on the more traditional mission work of sending missionaries and starting churches. Denominational missionaries declined, and non-denominational missionaries increased all around the world. As a result, missions became the work of specialized non-denominational organizations which only sent missionaries (Ott, Strauss, and Tennent 2010, 205–8). *Moreover, denominations, by sending help and not missionaries, became increasingly disconnected from the mission fields.*

What are some ways you think missions can become entangled with other people's motives? What impact do you think this can have on sending missionaries?

Missionaries inevitably arrive with their culture, but the challenge for the missionary is to understand the mission field's culture and to find ways to fit the gospel into that culture. The missionary, as Christ demonstrated, seeks to be the Word of the gospel through incarnation (in the flesh). The missionary joins the community to share in the burdens of the people and to bring hope. As missionaries to the Middle East, Andres and Angelica Guzman explained, "We lived among them as disciples of Christ" (Winter et al. 2009, 701).

Mission Concept: For the gospel to flourish in a new culture, it cannot be a culture transplanting its culture as if that is the gospel.

The Protestant Reformation did not separate the church from the state. However, the Reformation produced an opportunity for a new mission movement within the church. This movement was the Christian Anabaptist and Pietist movements, which refused to affiliate with any state church. This group rejected infant baptism, in part, because it was used to establish state citizenship (Pierson 2009, 154). Consequently, the state and state church questioned the patriotism of the Anabaptist and Pietist, which lead to their persecution. The Protestants were among the first to send out missionaries to proclaim Christ and not affiliate the new believers with a state church. Some of these persecuted Christians migrated to the American colonies and established churches with no state affiliation. The separation of the church from the state became the foundation of US American Christianity. Protestant missions also allowed American Christianity the opportunity to develop within its own cultural context, producing American Christianity with its own cultural styles.

Discussion. What are ways that the church can protect itself from the influence of political and secular forces that want to use the church for their own purposes?

THINK

One of the more famous Anabaptist groups were the Moravians. This group of early Protestants was formed in Moravia (today the Czech Republic) in 1722. They were an underground religious group persecuted by the Catholic Church. They were invited to live under the protection of a Lutheran nobleman named Nicolaus Zinzendorf. This group moved to what is today eastern Germany. Thus, by moving, they escaped the church and state partnership that persecuted them. They formed a Protestant Christian community. They were very devoted Christians. Their community grew to 300 people. They soon began to send out missionaries, and all were laymen. Their missionaries were Christian tradesmen that used their skills to make a living, and they established churches. These churches had no affiliation with any state. These churches accepted the cultural forms and styles of the culture where the church was located. Within 30 years, the Moravians of eastern Germany had sent hundreds of missionaries all over the world, including North and South America, the Caribbean, Africa, and Asia. The Moravians even established a church in the British colony of New York in North America.

The Moravian were the first wave of modern missions. What were the advantages of lay missionaries (non-clergy) who had trade skills? What were the advantages of missions that was focused on personal conversion? How do you think these missionaries changed the focus of missions?

Action: Do a web search on the Moravians. Read about the history of this early missionary movement.

The Princeton Theological Seminary missions professor Darrel Guder warns that evangelism can mistakenly be used to expand the church's culture, and not proclaim the gospel of Jesus Christ (2000, 190–91). When missions is centered on the church, it tends to create a gospel that is very similar culturally to the sending church. Therefore, missions can lead to absorbing other cultures into our culture so that we are alike. If we dress, sing, and talk the same, we must all be Christians. The problem with church-centered missions is the church does missions to benefit the church. The church that looks the same mistakenly believes it has succeeded as a church. In order to accomplish conformity, the church finds itself on a mission of dominance. This approach is the reverse of missionary incarnation; the mission field is forced to become like the missionary (and the sending church). When this happens, the church is expanding, but not the gospel. The gospel then becomes foreign and irrelevant to the mission field. This insight is what the Gentiles were trying to explain to the First Century Jewish Christians; the gospel needed to be separated from Jewish cultural forms and dressed in Gentile clothes for it to be relevant. The missionary needed to understand the culture of the mission field and help those people adapt the gospel to their culture. The early Jewish Christians agreed and made decisions that opened the world to the gospel.

Discussion. After looking at the scriptures of this study and the ideas presented so far, how do you understand evangelism?

THINK

There are currently twenty non-European countries in the world that have adopted Spanish, a European language, as their official language. Many of these countries are half a world away from Spain. Most declared the Roman Catholic Church their nation's church and Catholicism the official religion. The indigenous people in these countries adopted a European language and Western religious rituals.

The cathedrals of Latin America look like the cathedrals of Europe. Until the mid-1900s, they all used the same language, Latin. In some cases, this approach of sharing the gospel worked well enough. In other cases, Christianity was so foreign that the indigenous peoples rejected it or changed Christianity to such an extent that it was no longer Christianity. For example, the celebrations and prayers to the Virgin of Guadalupe in Mexico, a Catholic ritual, has its origin in the Aztec female deity's temple that was replaced with a Catholic cathedral.

Discussion. In what ways does church-centered missions drive missions out of the church? In what ways does it drive people away from the gospel?

Action: Do a web search on the Virgin of Guadalupe (Our Lady of Guadalupe), and a search on the Basilica of Guadalupe. Look at the origin of the celebrations of this virgin.

Mission Concept: For the gospel to spread throughout the world, it has to be relevant to the culture where it is proclaimed.

The Presbyterian mission leader and professor Paul Pierson observes that church renewal is often a case of the church rediscovering what it has forgotten (2009, 6). The New Testament church knew that missionaries were to spread the gospel message to all nations and allow the gospel to be adapted into the different cultures where it was planted. The church was diverse and one in Christ. Expansion was inseparable from a relational connection. However, as a result of Roman leaders accepting Christianity as the religion of Rome, the church became encumbered with political power and the practice of institutional domination. The church lost its way and mistakenly thought that Christianity had to look the same all over the world; and that all Christians had to express allegiance and devotion to the institutional church. Because of the Protestant Reformation, the church rediscovered what it had once known. The gospel can be expressed in different languages and in different cultural styles. More importantly, the Protestant Church emphasized that all Christians had a voice, not just the church's bishops and priests. This reality opened the door for the church to go to the mission field, proclaim Christ, disciple new believers, and then listen to what the new believers had to say about God. The church is a multicultural family in dialogue, and missions is how it becomes this church.

Discussion. As you think about Acts and the New Testament, are there concepts and ideas you think the church today needs to rediscover?

Looking ahead: In the next lesson, we will look at how the church imitates God when it does missions. The Trinity is foundational to missions, and it defines the church. The next lesson explains why the Trinity is indispensable to missions.

Reflection: Do a web search and find the words to the old Moravian hymn, *"Christian Hearts, in Love United."* Nicholas Zinzendorf wrote this hymn in the early 1700s. He was the wealthy noble that provided a haven for the Moravian Protestants. Read the hymn and think about the messages found in the words.

Day Three: The Trinity, The Foundation of Everything

Introduction: The Trinity is a profound Christian concept. This lesson will explain how the Trinity shapes and informs all aspects of missions. The foundational idea behind the Trinity is that God is three persons, and the Godhead is a loving and expanding fellowship. We will explore what this means to you as far as how you understand your church and its mission.

Scripture Review: Matthew 3: 13-17

In verse 14, John the Baptist was perplexed as to why Jesus requested baptism. John explained that he should be the one baptized by Jesus. Jesus then clarified that his request for baptism was related to God's standards. God desires righteousness. Sin separated humankind from God. Sin created relational brokenness at all levels of human relationships.

Pastor and professor Darrell Johnson reasons that "righteousness" is based on relational connectedness. He argues that reconciliation is the process of being re-connected and brought into fellowship (2002, loc. 685). The righteous are reconnected. Jesus, at his baptism, acknowledged the importance of repentance as the means to healing. Jesus was not baptized as a sinner; he was baptized as a messenger to announce the way of reconciliation with God and to each other. Baptism is a sign of reconnection. The Gospel of Matthew launches Jesus' ministry with baptism and concludes his earthly ministry with the Great Commission (Matthew 28). Jesus commands his disciples to go into all the world, make disciples and baptize them in the name of the Father, Son, and Holy Spirit. Baptism is a sacrament that announces a covenant between a person and God. As in marriage, a covenant is used to define the significance of the relationship between a man and a woman. By baptism in the name of the Father, Son, and Holy Spirit, the believer accepts God's offer to repent and be included into God's family and covenant of grace.

One can see in verses 16 and 17 that at Jesus's baptism, the three persons of the Trinity were introduced. Amazingly the witnesses of Jesus' baptism at the Jordan river saw God in God's fullness. Three things happened that revealed God's personhood: the Father spoke in an audible voice, the Son was there in the flesh, and the Holy Spirit was revealed in a mystical and visible way descending on Jesus (Lewis and Demarest 1996, Vol. 1, 262). The account of Jesus' baptism concluded with the Father professing that Jesus was His son, Jesus was beloved, and the Father was pleased.

This baptism account in the Bible demonstrates salvation is found in repentance and in relatedness. Baptism is inclusion into the Trinity and into the actions of the Trinity. Thus, salvation is found through a relationship with God. The Brazilian theologian Leonard Boff explains the Trinity is God's church, and we are an extension of that church (2000, 44, 66–67). The church is an expression of the Godhead, a loving community, a family that is on a mission from God. The church "is" God's love sent into creation to reconcile and connect creation. The manifestation of salvation is a diverse community living in peace with God and with each other. The church is attempting to rescue what sin has broken by forming both a local and global community (Harper and Metzger 2009, 155).

Discussion. The New Zealand theologian Adam Dodds explains that Jesus centered righteousness is not centered on written codes and rules to follow, but on attitudes and actions that establish a fellowship, a community (Dodds 2017, 24). Based on Jesus' baptism, how do you see God setting the stage for relationships as the basis of God's Kingdom?

Mission Concept: Missions is connectional, and it involves the church proclaiming the gospel and forming global relational connections.

In the early 20th Century, the Swiss theologian Karl Barth presented a new understanding about the church and its mission. His perspective was missions was not church centered; missions was God centered. The basis for missions, explained Barth, was the Trinity (Bosch 2011, loc. 9448). The Trinity, as the foundation for missions, inspired theologians and mission leaders to reconsider the church's motive for doing missions. The question was no longer: what was the church's mission and what was best for the church? The question shifted to: what was God's mission? Theologians realized that in order to answer that question it was important to understand God's nature.

THINK

When the church is focused on itself, that is called ecclesiocentrism *(ecclesio means "church' and centrism means "self-focus"). If missions is about what is best for the church, in particular the sending church, then missions is self-focused – ecclesiocentric.*

How does it happen that the church goes on its own mission and not God's mission? How do church leaders hold the church to God's mission?

Look at the Acts 13 story about Paul and Barnabas being sent from the Antioch Church. What captures the imagination is the image of church leaders laying hands on these two missionaries and sending them. What might be overlooked is the Bible clearly states, "the Holy Spirit said, 'set apart for me Barnabas and Saul [Paul] for the work to which I have called them'" (Acts 13: 2 ESV). It was not the Antioch Church that sent the first two missionaries; it was God. The church affirmed God's call and commissioned the missionaries. The church was affirming God's mission by sending two remarkable leaders. A self-serving church would not have sent two of its star leaders to distant lands. The church sent itself when it sent its own just as God did by sending Jesus and the Holy Spirit.

As noted above in the history of missions and the history of the church, we see the tendency to do things that are self-serving. If the growth and the success of the church as an institution is its mission, the church is selfish. Self-centeredness damages community. Sacrifice, as the Trinity demonstrates by sending Christ, is an expression of selfless love. And love is transformative and motivating when it is selfless. In trinitarian missions the "other" person or culture becomes the object of attention and devotion, not oneself.

God's mission will have aspects and characteristics of God. His mission is loving and sacrificial, and it brings people together into a new community while celebrating the diversity of cultures. The church is in the image of the Trinity and should be an example of God's nature.

Discussion. Can you think of some examples of "ecclesiocentrism" that you have seen or experienced?

THINK

In the early 1900s, World War I produced a theological crisis. When Christian nations dispatched troops to kill soldiers from other Christian countries, world war revealed something was wrong. The state was clearly expressing territorial dominance, and the state church was expected to be patriotic and supportive of the state's militarism. In many cases, the state church complied and dutifully prayed for their Christian young men to kill other Christian young men successfully. Church leaders realized something was horribly wrong and evaluated the church and missions. Leaders realized that the Western church was not extending the gospel of reconciliation around the world; it was championing state/cultural supremacy.

Why does the church become blindly associated with secular powers (state, political parties) that desire dominance and control of others?

Action: Do a web search on the Lutheran pastor Dietrich Bonhoeffer and note how he as a Christian in Germany opposed Nazism. He was martyred as a result of his criticism of Hitler.

Mission Concept: Shifting missions to the Trinity gives the church a mission and a purpose bigger than itself. The Trinity explains the nature of the church.

The understanding of the Trinity establishes a new and inspirational motivation for missions. The following is a list of concepts that theologians and mission leaders formed that highlight the Trinity's relationships to missions, and that reveal the nature of God.

- The Father sent His Son and the Holy Spirit into the world to bring healing. Jesus Christ was the first missionary sent by God. The initiator of missions is God, who calls and sends. As God sent His beloved Son to the mission field, so does the church send their beloved to the mission field.
    - The nature of God: God sends God's self into the world.
- The motivation for sending was love for the lost, and the cost was the sacrifice of a beloved son. Therefore, one can conclude that missions is sacrificial.
    - The nature of God: God sacrifices as an expression of love.
- The Trinity is a community of love and admiration. Love never takes place in solitude, and it requires relationships. God relates to humankind because God's nature, as seen in the Trinity, is relational. The early church theologian Augustine said, "There is no love where nothing is loved" (Augustine 2014, 195). The Father, Son, and Holy Spirit are love because they are a community in love. Love cannot exist in solitude. The words "God is love" have meaning because of the Trinity. God's plan is that humankind be invited to join the Trinity's community. Missions involves the formation of intercultural loving relationships. The church has to be global to reflect that God's Kingdom is relational in its focus and transcends all ethnicities, kingdoms, races, and nations.
    - The nature of God: God is relational, and God's Good News is about relationships that transcend cultural differences.
- The church, after Christ's ascension into heaven, was born from the Holy Spirit (see Acts 2). The church is empowered by God's Spirit and sent into the world to bring the lost back to God's Kingdom. The church is on God's mission, not its own mission. The church shows the world God's trinitarian relational nature and transformative power by how Christians form communities (churches) and love each other in visible and tangible ways.
    - The nature of God: God is a giver, giving Christians the Holy Spirit so that they can touch lives in meaningful ways.
- The early church leaders explained that God is One, yet the three persons in the Godhead indwell each other. The early church used the Greek word *perichoresis* [peri-cho-re-sis] to explain how something can be one, and also a mix of several things. A ray of light is a good example: it is white, but when refracted, it is a rainbow of color. As to color, one observes that a ray of light is one color, and at the same time, many colors. If a person knows Jesus, because of this indwelling, they know God. The Trinity is a community of inter-dwelling. The church, through the Holy Spirit, is part of this inter-dwelling. The church is remarkable because, although culturally diverse, it is made one by the Holy Spirit. Missions is a demonstration of the love of

Christ, realized in the hearts of Christians, that transcends all cultures thus allowing them to unite.

  - The nature of God: God is ONE in three persons, a fellowship in which each person is inter-dwelling in the other.

- The Trinity explains the importance of unity and diversity. God's nature is known through the diversity of the Trinity. The love between the Father, Son, and Holy Spirit produces revelations about the nature of God. As each in the Trinity adores and sacrifices for each other, each person of the Trinity is made known. The most profound truth comes from loving relationships. Through the relational community of the Trinity, God is revealed. In the same way, the church is a means of revelation. The church proclaims through word and sacraments the gospel message. The gospel, when planted in different cultures, through relational connections brings new revelations about God.
  - The nature of God: God is revealed and knowable through the Trinity and relatedness.
- Revelations about God are transformative. Barth, using the trinitarian model, explained that God was the revealer, the revelation, and the effect of the revelation (Barth and Johnson 2019, 126). The church and its culturally diverse disciples interact, and they gain revelations about God through interaction, and the entire church is transformed. Missions revitalizes the church.
  - The nature of God: Through relatedness God can transform lives.

Action: Take a moment to look over each bullet point and replace the words "God" with the words "the church." Then read the highlighted bullet point to understand the church and its mission better.

The church is made in the image of God. We are Christ's Church and a witness for Jesus Christ. Empowered by the Holy Spirit, the Church is the body of Christ in the world. Paul and John refer to the church as the bride of Christ (Ephesians 5:25, Revelations 19: 7-9, 21:2). The church's mission is defined by God's nature. The above list not only defines the nature of God, but it also reveals the nature and purpose of the church. The church is sent, it sacrifices, it builds community, it gives its power, it is a community that is diverse and unified, it reveals God, and it transforms lives.

Discussion. Based on the Trinity, why does the church have to do missions?

As a result of sending missionaries, the church is interconnecting around the world. Missions produces a global community. Leslie Newbigin, a mission leader, explains the role of the global church. The relational connecting, with God and each other, is the mission of

God's church. Newbigin adds that if we as a church proclaim Christ as reconciliation, and yet the church is divided into cultural camps, it discredits the witness of the church. The world sees the church as broken and separated (Newbigin and Weston 2006, loc. 1280). The church is to be the Trinity, a global community that is one, and at the same time, culturally diverse. The Trinity allows those in the church to retain their cultural uniqueness and, at the same time, be one in Christ. God's mission is reconciliation and oneness while we all retain our uniqueness.

Discussion. What do you think are some of the benefits the church gains through intercultural relationships and cultural diversity?

Looking ahead: One of the benefits of the Trinity as the basis of missions is that this concept explains the intensity of relationships God desires for the church. The following lesson talks about missions as an expression of relational intimacy and global connectedness.

Reflection: Find the Apostles Creed, read it, and think about what it says. This creed was the result of the church affirming the Trinity and explaining the person of Jesus Christ.

Day Four: The Witness of The Church Is Demonstrated by Global Connections

Introduction: When thinking about relationships and friendship, the Trinity presents the idea of intimacy. This lesson will look at what it means to be in a meaningful relationship with other people. Your church is to be a fellowship, a family, but more importantly - a global family. You will gain a vision for how missions can bring a new level of intimacy to your life.

Scripture Review: John 17: 20-26

The Vietnamese Catholic priest Van Nam Kim explains how trinitarian theology is limited when seen from a personal (psychological) perspective and not from a community (sociological) perspective. Self-awareness is the basis of psychological understanding (Kim 2014, 49–52). The Trinity, explains Kim, is not psychological, which is "to" and "with" one another. The Trinity is "in" one another – thus sociological. "In" one another, explains Kim, is based on a Greek word used in the 4th Century to explain the Trinity. The Trinity is a "*perichoresis*" (inter-dwelling) relationship where the group contains and interprets each other in the context of being different (2014, 51). The intimacy (inter-dwelling) of the three persons in the Godhead, is what makes them one. Kim expands on this to say that God creates a community with this *perichoresis* characteristic. He illustrates this in scripture, "That they may all be one, just as you, Father, are in me, and I in you, that they also may be in us, so that the world may believe that you have sent me" (John 17:21 ESV). Thus, God is revealed to the world through the relationship of the Trinity. Jesus reveals the Father and the Holy Spirit, and they reveal Jesus. And God extends love to the world because God knows love by being loved and loving.

Discussion. The Perichoresis idea is found in marriage. The Bible teaches the two shall become one (Matthew 19:5). When thinking about marriage, what does that mean to you?

John 17 presents Jesus's prayer before his death and resurrection. In verse 20 Jesus explains his prayer is for both his current and future disciples. His hope, says verse 21, is that his disciples will all be one, as he is one with the Father. Then Jesus prays that this relational oneness will reveal to the world that God sent Jesus. The implication is that through the disciples' unity, which is remarkable only because of the church's cultural and racial diversity, the church is a witness to the world of a loving God. As Jesus explains, the Father loves the Son, and the Son loves the Father – they are One. In verse 22, Jesus reveals that the Father gave the Son glory. The Greek word for "glory" is *doxa,* which is the word the church uses as the root word for doxology (praises). The implication is oneness is nurtured through praises. The Father and Son praise each other. The disciples are to be "like" the Father and the Son. In verse 23, Jesus expands on the *perichoresis* (inter-dwelling) concept. Jesus is in his disciples as God is in Jesus. The Holy Spirit resides in the hearts of the followers of Jesus, and because of the Holy Spirit, Jesus is in their hearts. The *perichoresis* idea means wherever the Holy Spirit is, so too are the Father and Son.

Action. Lookup the word "intimate." What does it mean to you to have an intimate relationship with God, with your family and those in your church?

The glue that connects all in unity is God's love flowing into Jesus, which flows into the disciples. This relationship is what Kim is talking about when he says *perichoresis* is to be a feature of the church. It is the inter-dwelling of the persons of the Trinity, which makes them one. And the church, indwelled by the Holy Spirit, proclaims God who is indwelling in Christians. In worship the church in community experiences God's love. As we worship, God flows from our hearts because God is in us. Verse 23 explains the result is perfect oneness. Perfect oneness is understood as love for each other and relational unity. In order to initiate this inter-dwelling with humankind Jesus came from God to this world. Jesus was beloved by his Father and willing to love. Verse 24 explains the intent of *perichoresis*, better yet, the motive for God sending. That fallen creation can be reconciled back to God through Jesus Christ and stand by his side as beloved brothers and sisters when the Father praises His Son. Through Christ, Christians have the privilege of standing with Christ and receiving the praises of the Father, like the bride of a beloved son. The intent of sending is to form relational connections that lead to a new community, one that God will praise and honor. In verse 25 we see this community of love is defined by those who know Jesus, which is not everyone in the world. This section of verses concludes with the *perichoresis* idea as it relates to love. In verse 26 Jesus prays saying he made God known and he will continue to make God known in the world. Jesus will do this so that all can see the depth of the Father's indwelling love in His Son and how much the Son's love indwells in his disciples. God's love is in the Son and the Son (through the Holy Spirit) is in his disciples. The Trinity and the disciples of Christ are in *perichoresis.* The love of God indwells in the followers of Jesus Christ. The love found in the Trinity flows into the church. The mission of God is that others come to know the indwelling of God in their lives and become One with each other and with God.

Discussion. After reading about ONENESS, what are some of your ideas regarding being one as a group/church?

THINK

At 17 years old, Julia Leavitt moved to Japan, sponsored by the Cumberland Presbyterian (CP) Women's Board of Missions. She was from Bloomfield, Indiana, and the first woman sent by the newly formed CP Women's Mission Board. When she arrived in Japan in 1881 by ship, CP missionaries met her. Julia was a quick study and mastered the Japanese language and culture. Julia eventually moved to the remote area of Tanabe as an evangelist. Other missionaries expressed fear about living in Tanabe; it was a remote stormy coastal fishing town, Julia went anyway.

In a conference in Tokyo in 1900, Julia expressed a concern. She noted that many missionaries in Japan were living in the same city. She asked the missionaries to move out of their missionary communities and into the cities and villages of Japan. Julie was an evangelist living among the Japanese. She was calling others to follow her footsteps. Julia had become somewhat famous for her remarkable Japanese and the fact she lived with the Japanese in places where there were no other missionaries. Other missionaries were often amazed when they visited her. They noted how involved and accepted she was by the Japanese. They all noted her stamina and personal sacrifice.

Julia noticed an all too common problem among Christians (among all people). We all like to be around people like ourselves. How can we break away from our culture group to join with people of a new culture? What keeps us from doing this?

Therefore, the new unity is diversity in communion. The Holy Spirit working within the church does not erase our distinctions and differences; in reality, the Spirit makes them non-divisive (Gaillardetz, 2008, 38). David Bosch explains that Christian unity is not a dialogue where there is a coming together of minds; unity is the coming together of hearts (2011, loc. 11358). Opinions, in the context of loving dialogue, are transformative. A person with an opinion and no dialogue is just opinionated. The inter-dwelling of God in the hearts of the followers of Christ produces unity and allows for cultural and racial diversity. The fact there is diversity, and still communion, speaks to the reality that God sent His Son into the world to bring reconciliation to broken relationships. If those who are culturally different can be ONE in Christ, then God is with us – Emmanuel.

Discussion. *What are some ways we can share our opinions and ideas with each other and maintain an open dialogue?*

Intercultural communication is a key factor in missions. The first challenge for the missionary is to learn the language of those the missionary seeks to serve. The second step is to understand their cultural perspective - how they see the world. Milton Bennet, a social anthropologist, explains we tend to understand other people based on our experiences. We organize our cultural understanding of a person based on how we understand our cultural reality (Bennett 2013, 47). This approach leads to stereotypes. If people in another culture are often late to an appointment, a Western culture assumes they are lazy. If people are direct in their communication, a Central American culture thinks they are rude. If people are independent and make decisions without group approval, an Asian culture assumes they are disrespectful.

Stereotypes lead to misinformation and misunderstandings. In order to understand a culture and its people, the missionary must become an insider, a friend. The first step is to overcome stereotypes. Everyone has a good reason for acting the way they do; the challenge is to understand the reason for their actions. The second step is a mutual commitment by both the missionary and those on the mission field to get to know each other. Becoming an insider is not possible if the missionary is not accepted into the community. Third, the missionary has to decide if they will change to accommodate the new culture and new friends. This factor has a major impact on a missionary being accepted into a new culture. Mission leaders often tell new missionaries that flexibility is key to mission work. Change often means listening and dialogue, adapting to new ways of doing things, withholding opinions, and depending on other people of a different culture. Nothing builds trust faster than dependence on another person. Insiders are trusted and trusting; that is why they are insiders. Reliance on those of another culture goes against the human desire to avoid risk. Being a cultural insider is born from these steps. It involves time, trust, and proximity. Friends spend time together, they are in physical proximity, and they take risks trusting each other. Meaningful friendships also involve disagreements, mistakes, misunderstandings, and above all - forgiveness (Moreau, Greener, and Campbell 2014, 241–50). These are some of the characteristics of the inter-dwelling of lives. The fellowship of Christ is a fellowship that celebrates Christ and lives in friendship with others.

Discussion. After reading the steps of becoming an insider, that is, intercultural friendship, take a moment to talk about how Jesus came to our world and what he did to become a friend of his disciples. Using the steps outlined, what are examples you think of where Jesus became the friend of sinners?

Mission Concept: Cultural diversity and harmony within the global church reveals Christ's power to reconcile humankind to God and to each other, and reconciliation implies being friends.

The Malaysian/American professor of theology Amos Yong explains that catholicity is needed to maintain the purity of the church. By diversity and communion (unity), there is holiness (2005, 132–33). Catholic means the whole church or the universal church. It was first used around 100 A.D. to describe the Christian Church. Between the 9th and 11th Century

Catholic became a term that referred to the Western Christian church based in Rome. Thus, catholic became part of the name of a religious denomination, the Roman Catholic Church. The British theologian N.T. Wright, states, "I think the word *Catholic* is far too good a word for the Romans to keep it all to themselves" (Green 2019). Catholicity speaks to a foundational concept of missions. Catholic means a relational connection that stretches far beyond our local community. Modern mission leaders refer to catholicity as the process of becoming a culturally diverse, yet unified Christian church. All denominations and mission agencies should aspire to be catholic. The scriptures from John 17 provide a great explanation of catholicity. Being catholic means Christians share their lives with each other to such an extent that there is unity of the body, yet we are all unique. Missions takes this sharing of lives to an international level. The Bible and the Holy Spirit instruct the church as to the actions and attitudes that allow for unity.

Discussion. Can you think of examples of catholicity in your community, a case where you have seen or experienced it?

Action: In the spirit of praise for others, share the name of a person you know and explain what you like about that person. Talk about a different culture you know and share positive things you see in that culture.

Looking Ahead: A common term used when talking about the church and missions is the expression "missional church." Many speakers and writers that talk about missions refer to this idea. In the next lesson we will explore what it means to be a missional church.

Reflection: Read the Old Testament book, *The Song of Solomon*. As you read this book think about intimacy and inter-dwelling. This book shows God's love for the church. Think about this book in relationship to the church and its mission of relational unity. Look at how the lover speaks and acts toward the one loved.

Day Five: The Missional Church, More Than a Mission Program

Introduction: Missions leads to cultural diversity, that is, people of different races and nationalities living in harmony. The idea of "missional" explains how we as Christians can surpass the limitations of our culturally simple lives and experience the vibrance and richness of intercultural relationships. This lesson explores why loving others is important to God's witness and how to practice love for others.

Scripture Review: Colossians 3: 11-15

The city of Colosse was the home of the Colossian Church. This church was probably a daughter church that was founded by Christians from Ephesus. The Colossian Church was primarily a Gentile church. Paul, while a prisoner in Rome, sent the Colossians a letter to encourage them and to help them refute heresies that were being circulated in the early church. Part of this letter illustrates the significance of missions in relation to unity and diversity.

In Colossians 3:11, Paul refutes the idea that a person must conform to cultural norms or practices before they can be a Christian. Some Jewish Christians insisted that Gentile Christians had to first be Jewish in norms and practices (circumcision and Jewish dietary laws) before they could become Christians. Paul explained there were no cultural standards to be a Christian. There were no Greek or Jew, circumcised or uncircumcised, cultural requirements to be a Christian. He then expanded the concept of diversity to include Gentile cultural realities that were produced by the expanding church. Paul added, there are no barbarians (non-Greeks) or Scythians (tribal people North of the Black Sea), or slaves and free people. All Christians are all in Christ regardless of ethnicity or social status. Paul did not tell Christians to lay aside their ethnic or social status; he said it was not necessary to become a different ethnicity or gain a different social status to be part of God's family. Paul's focus was on relational connections that transcend culture and social status. Paul's faith family was multi-national, and as he explained, forming this family was not easy. Paul affirmed cultural and socio-economic diversity in the church and disavowed cultural conformity in order to be a follower of Christ.

Discussion. What are some of the dynamics in the life of a family that cause tension in the family? A global faith family can also expect tensions, what attitudes should people in that family express to each other in order to live in peace?

Mission Concept: All cultures are learned and involve norms of behavior, social expectations, and unique styles, fashions, literature, foods, language, and music. A global faith family experiences both unity and the tensions of cultural diversity.

In Colossians 3:12, Paul explains the way unity works. Christians are chosen and beloved by God. They are included in God's Kingdom. They are part of the divine family, and as such, they too are holy. So, says Paul, express these attitudes with each other: Be kind, humble, meek, and patient with each other. Paul is providing some necessary attitudes that build friendships. In verse 13, he urges Christians to bear each other's burdens, share in the suffering of each other. If someone has been offended, forgive the offender as Jesus forgave us. Paul is explaining that in friendship, we make mistakes, but the relationships can be restored. These attitudes, of reconciliation, are in the context of verse 11, which explain Christian friendship is to include cultural and social diversity. The mission of God is offering humanity a means of reconciliation with God and with each other.

As the church expands into the world, it, too, is a platform for reconciliation. The church's power is seen in its loving global community. Love is more complicated than reciting creeds or participating in uniformed rituals. The church demonstrates God's nature and proclaims God's invitation to join God's Kingdom community, which is not based on a particular cultural style or form. In order to love as the Trinity loves, the followers of Christ have to change attitudes and behaviors. The Bible and the Holy Spirit teach and inspire those attitude changes. The church is then a local and global community demonstrating God's nature of unique personhood, reconciliation, and fellowship.

Discussion. Beliefs are important, and actions that lead to reconciliation and community are also important. What are some crucial beliefs the Bible teaches? What are some important actions (behaviors) the Bible teaches? How do beliefs and actions help us form meaningful relationships?

THINK

Missional means "being oriented toward mission in thinking, acting and living," placing missions as the "heartbeat" of the church (Pocock, Van Rheenen, and McConnell 2005, loc. 235). This common term is woven throughout books, articles, lectures, and sermons about missions. The concept had its origins in the early 1980s when the originators talked about the missional church in the context of cross-cultural missions (Ott and Netland 2006, 197).

The church is missional in two ways. First, it demonstrates reconciliation and community at the local level. The local church builds a meaningful community that is united in Christ. Community is not easy; faith family unity is never without tension. It is hard to develop and maintain attitudes that lead to sacrificial actions and service to others. The second way that the church is missional, the very foundation of the missional concept, is through reconciliation and community, which extends into the world. The idea of the missional church is that reconciliation starts locally, and it expands to include the global community. Community is not two things, local and global; it is one thing. The church is missional in that it does one thing; it proclaims the gospel of reconciliation and demonstrates the gospel of reconciliation, both near and far. The missional idea intended to see missions as what the church is, not as something the church does. The church's most faithful and most profound witness is its ministry of reconciliation spread around the world. The church shows unity in Christ amid cultural diversity. The church's mission proclaims the nature of God and the power of the gospel.

What can your church do to demonstrate both local and global reconciliation and community?

Action: Use a dictionary or use your own understanding of these words to define these attitudes: kindness, humility, meekness, patience.

In Colossians 3: 14 and 15, Paul presents the lifeblood of the Trinity, which is love. The Father, Son, and Holy Spirit profoundly love each other. Everything they do is for the benefit of the other.

Discussion. What are things you sacrificially do for your children, spouse, or a family member that demonstrates that they are more important than you? How can you apply the love you have experienced in your family to your church and to missions?

The Son submits to baptism and death on the cross because of his love for the Father. The Father sacrifices his beloved Son because of His love for creation. The Son says his only desire is to honor his Father. The Holy Spirit births the church so that it can honor the Son and worship him. The Son warns humanity not to offend the Holy Spirit. The Bible announces that the Father plans for all of creation to bow and honor His Son. Thus, says Paul, love binds everything together. Everything God is doing revolves around honoring the other through sacrifice. Trinitarian love is expressed as a sacrifice of self and honor for the other. The church finds harmony when it relies on the indwelling of the Holy Spirit and imitates the Trinity. The Trinity is sacrificial, and always working for the honor and glory of the other. The inter-dwelling of Christ in the heart of the believer is indispensable. It rules in the heart of the Christian and pushes the believer to honor God and others. The mission of God is that the world sees what God can do in the hearts of men and women by how they honor each other. The harmony found within diversity demonstrates God's love and the inter-dwelling of the Holy Spirit in the hearts of men and women.

Discussion. How can we share the burdens of Christians on the mission field? How can they share our burdens?

It is challenging to talk about missions without talking about poverty. Missions often involves sending missionaries to developing countries. A developing country is one that has a high level of poverty. Bryan Myers, a professor and staff person of World Vision International, explains some important aspects of poverty. Myers explains that most Christians (and people) think poverty is a deficit. Poor people lack food, housing, clothing, education, and knowledge. Seeing poverty this way means the appropriate response is the more affluent and better-educated respond to the poor with "provision." The problem with this perspective is it demeans the poor as inferior, and it aggrandizes the provider as superior. Myers explains that a better understanding is to see poverty as a result of broken relationships. Poverty involves being excluded, alone, marginalized, and abandoned. The poor are the outcasts who have limited access to those who are in strong communities that have stability and prosperity. Myers's innovative idea is to understand poverty is the result of relational separation. With this understanding the solution to poverty is relational connection, not just provision (Winter et al. 2009, 607–9). If missions is understood as relational connections that are a product of Christ and reconciliation, then missions has the ability to lift people out of poverty. The gospel then transcends culture and socioeconomic status. This lifting is not the result of shifting resources to the poor, which is needed but only leaves the poor with temporary relief; missions is much more. It is bringing the poor into the global church family. Missions is the missionary in relational connection, which is being a friend to the poor. Missions is the sending church being relationally connected with the mission field – which is more than just sending help.

Discussion. Think about the poor around you, how can you be more than a provider and be a friend of the poor? How can your church be a friend to the global poor?

Relational connections and forming community help clarify the mission idea of "redemption and lift." This mission theory, of the early 1980s, believed the gospel brings societal improvements, like schools, hospitals, literacy, and ethical values that improve a community - "lift." The gospel results in people, their families, and their communities, being more prosperous (McGavran and Wagner 1990, loc. 2615). Myers's idea gives redemption and lift a new perspective. The gospel can produce a more prosperous society because it brings people into relational connections within a healthy community. The community, in sacrificial love for each other, is able to lift each other. The "lift" comes through relationships that are formed as a family of faith. The missional church is the entire church in relational connections, both locally and globally. As Paul's letter to the Colossians explains, the faith family has to practice relational values that tie us together. Christians believe the Bible and the Holy Spirit assists the believer in making the changes necessary to live in fellowship with others.

Mission Concept: Love is more than proclaiming the gospel of Christ, it is acceptance, fellowship, and sharing each other's burdens. In the case of the mission field, missions gives us a way to cross cultural barriers, form multicultural communities and share each other's burdens.

Action: Think of a mission field that you know. Then make a list of what you think their burdens are and what you can do to share those burdens. Then pray and ask God what you should do.

Looking ahead: The next lesson will explore how to evaluate when we are successful in missions. The church has often been fooled into thinking increased numbers is how to evaluate success, as you will see, the Trinity shows the church what success looks like.

Reflection: Look at Matthew 25: 31-46. Jesus talks about the hungry, the naked, the sick, and the imprisoned. Look closely at these verses and see if you can identify the "relational" aspects of what Jesus is telling his disciples to do with these people in need. Look at Leviticus 19: 33-34 to understand the relational challenge God gave the Israelites with respect to other cultures.

Day Six: The Doxology, Doing One Thing Well

Introduction: The challenge before the church is how to evaluate that the church is effectively doing mission work. We all need a means to evaluate our mission work so that we can be certain we are on God's mission and not our own mission. In this lesson we will discover how we can assess the effectiveness of the mission of our church.

Scripture Review: Acts 13:44-50

These verses are a continuation of Paul and Barnabas' first missionary journey. They first visited Cyprus, then they took a boat and sailed on to what is today southern Turkey. They traveled by land on to a town called Antioch of Pisidia (different than the city where the Antioch Church was located). This town was in the province of Galatia, and the churches established in this province eventually received a letter from Paul – Galatians. Paul and Barnabas entered a Jewish synagogue and shared the Gospel. They then moved into the streets of Antioch to share the gospel.

Verses 44-46 report that because of the street ministry, the next Sabbath resulted in a large Gentile crowd at the synagogue to hear Paul. The Gentile presence in the synagogue annoyed the Jews; first, they were crowding out the normal attendees, and second, they were sympathetic to Paul's message about Jesus Christ. Some Jews accepted Paul's message, but the majority did not. The Jewish majority rose-up and denounced Paul's message. Verse 46 records that Paul explained the Jews had been given first rights to the gospel, and if they rejected it, the Gentiles were next in line to hear. This experience illustrated a pattern seen throughout Paul's missionary ministry, Jews largely rejected the gospel message, and Gentiles were more favorable to the message.

In verse 47, Paul referenced the prophet Isaiah as a way to help the Jews understand their role. They were to be a light to the Gentiles. The Jews understood this to mean the Gentiles were to convert to Judaism. If the Gentiles accepted Judaism, they were accepted as converts to Judaism (called "proselytes"). Paul was trying to explain that this verse was related to Jesus Christ, a Jew, being Good News to the Gentiles. Paul's idea of conversion was a commitment to Jesus Christ.

The Gentiles, in their excitement, started to glorify the Word of Jesus Christ. As Paul and Barnabas explained Christ's message of Good News, the crowds grew in number and in praises for Jesus Christ (verses 48-49). Verse 50 says the enthusiasm resulted in the Gentiles spreading out into Galatia to tell their stories. The gospel message exploded into the town and surrounding area.

Discussion. How did worship impact the Gentiles in Antioch? What impact did it have on the Jews and civic leaders in Antioch? What does this tell you about worship?

Action: Tell about a worship service you saw or were involved in that resulted in enthusiasm. Talk about how you saw that enthusiasm motivate those in attendance.

The impact of Paul's message on the Gentiles was dramatic. They were enthusiastic converts to the gospel of Christ. The Jews of Antioch, in particular the Jewish women who were probably married to Gentile civic leaders, complained about Paul and Barnabas. Eventually, the city leaders ordered Paul and Barnabas to leave (verse 50).

When reading this story, how does one evaluate the missionary's work? Paul and Barnabas did preach, and lots of people came to faith in Christ. But they offended the Jews and frightened the civic leaders and were exiled from the city. At best, the missionaries split the synagogue, some Jews did believe in Christ. At worst, they created a riot of enthusiasm for Jesus Christ that resulted in their persecution.

Discussion. If you were Paul and Barnabas's mission director and you were evaluating their work, what would your report say?

THINK

In the 1920s, a farmer in the remote Andes Mountains of Colombia traveled to a nearby town to shop. While in the market, he bought a Bible. The farmer took it back to the farm and read it by the light of his new gas lantern. After reading some of the words, he decided to invite the Bible salesman to his farm to explain the Bible. The salesman, a Christian, came and spent a week on the remote farm. The salesman explained what the Bible was and shared the gospel. During that week, over 30 people came to faith in Christ. The Bible salesman instructed the new believers to read the Bible. The families impacted by the gospel met together, read the Bible, and sang songs they wrote about what they were reading. These new believers started to share their faith with other families on remote farms. Within a few months, they reported over 100 people in attendance at their Bible study and worship service. Eventually, missionaries were told about this group and missionaries visited them to explain in greater depth the stories of the Bible. This group grew and over the years produced many churches and many church leaders. The number of people who came to Christ and the number of churches founded in Colombia because of what happened on that farm in the 1920s is beyond measure. (This account was taken from the book, *Eloisa en El Umbral del Infinito*, by Samaria Marque Jaramillo.)

What do you think worship should involve? What are some elements of worship that create enthusiasm for the gospel?

Mission Concept: Question 1. *What is the chief end of man?* Answer. Man's chief end is to glorify God and to enjoy him forever. *Westminster Shorter Catechism*, 1647 A.D.

In the 1600s, the Protestant Dutch professor Gisbertus Voetius gave the world his understanding of what missions involves. Voetius was an early Protestant church leader. He recognized that God sends and is the first cause of missions. He also recognized that the church is sent, the second cause of missions (Ott and Netland 2006, 82). He then answered the question of what the "sent" are supposed to do. Professor Voetius explained that missions was threefold in purpose: it was to evangelize, it was to plant churches, and it was to be "doxological" (Paas 2016, 23–24).

Action. Read the old hymn many churches sing called "The Doxology" (1674). What do the words of this short song ask us to do?

This third purpose of missions is an intriguing concept. *Doxology* means to say praises, in particular, to praise or glorify God. "The glory of God is the crowning purpose to which conversion and church planting contribute" (Ott and Netland 2006, 82). In other words, all roads of missions lead to God's glorification. Missions is to lead humankind to glorify God. In the Gospel of John, chapters 15 and 16, Jesus explains to his disciples his love for the Father. As the Father has loved the Son, the Son loves the disciples. Jesus explains in John 15 that those who honor Jesus are also honoring the Father. Clearly, Jesus prioritizes glorifying the Father. Both Jesus and the Holy Spirit seek to call men and women to worship God (John 14: 21-24). Jesus prayed, "Father, the hour has come, glorify your Son, that the Son may glorify you" (John 17: 1 ESV).

John Piper, an American theologian and writer explains, "Missions is not the ultimate goal of the church. Worship is. Missions exists because worship doesn't." Piper concludes, "Worship, therefore, is the fuel and goal of missions" (Piper 2010, 11). The book of Revelation well explains the end game; God is worshiped by angels and all human tribes and nations (Revelation 7 and 19). In fact, the goal of missions is simple. It is to bring people into a relationship with Jesus Christ and guide them (discipleship) to be part of a community that worships God. Where there is worship, the task of missions is accomplished. Worshiping our loving and sacrificial God is not only the right thing to do; it is also transformative. Worship changes us and changes our world. The Acts 13 account shows that the Gentiles, and some Jews, were proclaiming praises to Jesus Christ. They were worshiping the Lord. Their lives were changing, and their community took notice.

The seminary professor Amos Yong (Fuller Seminary) explains that the practices of worship, prayer, and praise, are ways Christians impact the world around them. Worship brings the power of the Holy Spirit into confrontation with the powers of the world, both demonic and political powers (Yong 2010, 152). In Acts 12, Peter was jailed, and it was through the church's worship that the doors were opened, and Peter walked free. This account from the Bible shows worship had a physical impact on a bad situation. This is Yong's point; worship has the power to change things for the better. The first missionary journey, seen in Acts 13, was the result of worship. Even the sending of missionaries was born from worship.

Discussion. Have you seen or experienced worship changing a bad situation?

Action: *Can you think of other stories or accounts in the Bible where there was worship and worship had an impact on the community?*

The mission concept of the Doxology is the first article of the *Westminster Larger Catechism*, developed initially as a teaching tool for Christians in the mid-1600s. Using questions as a way to teach doctrine, the *Catechism* asks, "What is the highest and chief end of man?" It answers, "Man's chief and highest end is to glorify God, and fully to enjoy him forever." The Doxology explains that missions exists for the purpose of God's glorification. As a result of this concept, the church and its missionaries can evaluate their effectiveness by asking if their mission efforts have resulted in God's glorification. Indeed, when missionaries develop new worshiping communities, they are fulfilling the reason for being sent.

Worship is more than singing a few songs; it is a community living in devotion, compassion, sacrifice, and acts that are pleasing to God (Ott and Netland 2006, 84). As Jesus explained to his disciples, "In the same way, let your light shine before others, so that they may see your good works and give glory to your Father who is in heaven" (Matthew 5:16 ESV). Our service to humanity, through works of righteousness, is to produce God's glorification. This verse is in the context of the Sermon on The Mount, at the end of the beatitudes. One of the most important parts of this sermon is the beatitudes (Matthew 5: 1-12). The beatitudes and other parts of the sermon are related to deeds and attitudes which build relationships. Thus, worship is prayers and songs in honor of Jesus Christ, the Father, and the Holy Spirit. And worship is also deeds that reflect the nature of God. Blessed are the poor in spirit, blessed are those that morn, blessed are the meek, blessed are those that hunger for righteousness, blessed are the merciful; these statements are all relational concepts. God's nature is relational, and the deeds of God's followers promote relationships, even repairing broken relationships. Piper adds that "the white-hot worship of God and his Son among all the peoples of the earth," is the goal and "missions is the means" (Piper 2010, loc. 602). Where there is worship, there is success.

Discussion. If you were sent to the mission field to evaluate how successful the missionaries and new mission churches were, what are the things you would want to see?

Mission Concept: Where God is glorified, missions is successful. Where there is worship, there is transformation.

The Holy Spirit, through the worship of the Antioch Church, dispatched the first missionaries. When they arrived in Southern Turkey, they proclaimed the gospel of Jesus Christ and established a worshiping community. The gospel spread in word and deed and was propelled from street to street, village to village through the inspiration of worship. If the missionaries would have stayed in the synagogue arguing, they would not have had an impact on the city. However, by going into the streets and sharing the gospel and leading the Gentiles in the worship of Jesus Christ, the resulting zeal for God was transformative. Worship was power, and it had the power to change lives. The synagogue leaders and the civil authorities were rightly concerned; their community was changing because of worship.

Action: Talk about things you would like to see in your own life with respect to worship. Talk about what you would like to see in your church as far as worship.

Looking ahead: The next lesson will explore how missions produces wisdom. Missions has benefits not only for the mission field, but also for the missionary, the sending church, and the global Christian Church. Through missions, God reveals God's kingdom.

Reflection: Look at the beatitudes in Matthew 5: 2-12. All are related to attitudes and actions related to building healthy relationships. Look at each one and in your own words (written or verbal) describe how that beatitude reveals how to treat other people. These actions should be considered acts of worship.

Day Seven: Missions, the Road That Reveals God's Kingdom

Introduction: Missions is much more than taking the gospel to a foreign land. In fact, missions reveals things to us about God that we could never know without our church being on God's mission. This lesson will explain the importance of missions as a source of God's message to your church. You will realize that missions can open your eyes to new things about God.

Scripture Review: I Corinthians 1: 18-31

Corinth, of the New Testament, was a major city in southern Greece. It was a city of commerce; culturally, it was strongly Roman and Greek. The city was also international with immigrants from many cultures. As was Paul's custom when on missionary trips, he first connected with the Jews in the city by visiting the synagogue (Acts 18: 3-4). He then networked out of the synagogue into the city evangelizing Gentiles and Jews. Typically, he was more successful with the Gentiles than with the Jews. The end result of his missionary journey to Corinth was the formation of a church. The two letters to the Corinthians are letters to the believers of Corinth.

These verses in I Corinthians 1 talk about wisdom. "Where is the one who is wise?" (I Corinthians 1: 20 ESV). Corinth was a city that saw itself as a community of intellectuals. Paul explained that God's wisdom was not the world's wisdom, in fact, "analytical thought" could not discover God (I Corinthians 1:21).

A philosopher using deductive reasoning or a scientist using experiments will not find God. Paul points out an important cultural dynamic, different cultures gain wisdom in different ways. The Greeks and Romans used deductive reasoning as the source of wisdom. The Jews used observation.

Discussion. Different personalities learn in different ways, as do cultures. Are you a visual, auditory, or tactile learner?

The Bible explains that the Jews were looking for manifestations, signs and wonders; to validate truth. It is similar to the idea that all rich people must be intelligent and talented, how else could they become rich? Thus, worldly wisdom says that all rich people are wise, and all poor people are not wise. This reflects the idea that the effects of wisdom can be observed. Then Paul points out that the Greeks seek logic to gain wisdom. They are the philosophers, and their wisdom is based on logical arguments that win people over to their view (see Acts 17:21). This concept is like a politician presenting their ideas and winning people over to accept those ideas and vote for the person. Wisdom is then a good idea that people like. Wisdom is accepting ideas that seem proven. Paul's conclusion: the gospel of Jesus Christ is not acceptable for Jews or Greeks. The Jews cannot imagine Christ dying on the cross and being the "Christ." This is contrary to those who promote the idea that the righteous and chosen should not suffer. Only sinners suffer. And the Greeks find it illogical that God would come as a man, die on the cross and return from the dead. Is it reasonable to believe that the dead return to life? Paul responds, "the foolishness of God is wiser than men" (I Corinthians 1: 25 ESV).

Discussion. Why do you think wisdom is incomplete or untrue when it is based on what we experience or based on what the majority finds acceptable?

Action: Read the story about Simon in Acts 8: 8-24 and reflect on how he was confused by his supernatural experiences. Read the story of Paul in Athens and reflect on how those in the Athens Temple gained their wisdom (Acts 17: 16-21). In one case, supernatural experiences (Acts 8) resulted in confusion, and in the other case, in-depth study and discussion lead to uselessness (Acts 17).

Mission Concept: Different cultures gain wisdom in different ways. For Christians, salvation is not found in what we know; it is found in who we know.

Paul then makes the connection between wisdom and a relationship with God. In verse 26, Paul refers to the calling of the Christians in Corinth. It is through their relationships with Jesus Christ that they are made wise. Their wisdom is not based on the standards of the world. It is not wealth, power, or applause that makes a person wise (verses 26-27). Even the marginalized poor, powerless, and unknown can be wise in Christ (I Corinthians 1: 28-29). It is the relationship that produces wisdom, righteousness, sanctification, and redemption (verse 30). Therefore, Christians cannot boast about their wisdom because their wisdom and righteousness are based on who they know (verse 31).

Discussion. Who are people in your life that taught you things as a result of the relationship you had with them? What did they teach you?

THINK

The famous book Peace Child, by Don Richardson (Richardson 2005) is an example of how a missionary finds revelations from God on the mission field. Richardson identified a custom that New Guinea tribes used when at war with each other. These warring tribes exchanged a child to bring peace between the tribes. The child was the peace treaty. In the context of war and peace, Richardson understood this custom as the gospel of Jesus. Their tribal custom was a revelation about God. The "Divine" peace child, Jesus, was understandable and relevant to the New Guinea tribes. The New Guinea peace child allowed the missionary to gain an even deeper understanding of what God did by giving His only Son as a peace child. This account illustrates how the missionary is challenged with the task to discern, to become a cultural insider, and perceive the world as those on the mission field perceive the world (Hesselgrave and Rommen 2000, 150–51). The missionary, as the result of their relationship with people in New Guinea, gained wisdom about God's Kingdom.

What is something unique to your culture that you believe reveals the gospel message?

Mission Concept: Wisdom is found in relatedness, and with respect to missions, wisdom is found within intercultural relationships.

Saint Augustine, a 4th Century theologian, explains that isolation from others inhibits knowledge and relatedness increases knowledge (2014, 195–97). Solomon said the same in Proverbs; there is more wisdom in a group than from an individual (Proverbs 11:14, 15:22). Missions is not a one-way street in which the missionary teaches, and the mission field listens. Missions is the missionary proclaiming the gospel message and the mission field accepting the gospel, then explaining the gospel from their cultural perspective. These new cultural insights from the mission field about the gospel bring new revelations about God's Kingdom. Missions is a two-way street. The missionary shares the gospel, and the mission field helps the missionary understand new insights about God as they incorporate the gospel into their cultural context. The theory of general revelation, which is an idea of the Protestant Reformation, explains that God communicates God's existence, power, and glory to all humankind, and none are left without an excuse. God reveals God's self in various ways through Scripture, nature, and even people (Ott, Strauss, and Tennent 2010, 331–32). God can use people to reveal things about God's Kingdom.

Andrew Walls, a mission historian, gives this explanation about God's revelations through missions. Walls explains that the gospel is translated by each culture and examined through the eyes of that culture. This new cultural perspective impacts the church's understanding of the gospel (2006, 16). The cultural perspective does not change the gospel, it only reveals it in greater depth. For example, the gospel started among 1st Century Jews. The Jews were experiential, that is, they wanted to experience God. The disciples of Jesus and the numerous Jewish followers of Jesus learned about God by observing God's signs and wonders. Look at the many miracles that the Jews experienced in the Old and New Testament. The Jewish believers interpreted God's Kingdom as they experienced God. God is a God of actions to be experienced. God is understood through God's signs and wonders. God is not just an idea. The gospel then moved into the Greek and Roman context. For this culture what a person believed was important (Walls 2006, 17). Much of the theology we have today as Christians has its origin in the first few hundred years of the church, which was primarily located in the Roman Empire. The Romans helped the church understand concepts about God and the formation of appropriate beliefs.

Discussion. The gospel is increasing in South America and Africa and decreasing in Europe and North America. Based on this trend, in the future, most Christians will be found in the Southern Hemisphere. What did your culture add to Christian understanding that will be helpful to Christians in the Southern Hemisphere? What do you think the church will learn from the world's Southern Hemisphere (South America, Africa)?

When the gospel arrived in Europe, the cultures of Europe revealed new things about God's Kingdom. Protestants in Europe realized that there was a priesthood of all believers. European Christianity was more focused on individualism and equality. These Christians reveled that Christian faith is personal and that all men and women are capable of professing their faith in Christ and serving God (Walls 2006, 20). The European Protestants revealed that Christ was personal, and any person can be used by God, regardless of their status in society. These ideas are found throughout scripture, but because of the European cultural perspective, the early Protestants were sensitive to scriptures that revealed these truths.

As missionaries move the gospel into new cultures, these cultures see things that others do not see, and they reveal to the church new understandings about God. The mission professor Paul Hiebert explains that we are limited in fully understanding God because of our culture. There are things we just cannot see about God because of our culture (Hiebert 2008, loc. 5704). It is like we are taking a picture of a mountain range; the camera lens limits us from seeing the full panorama. Hiebert then explains that each culture also sees things that others do not see. For this reason, each culture needs to self-theologize. This means to think about scripture in light of their culture. Although limited by their culture in knowing everything, there are some things they are able to see that others do not see (Hiebert 1987, 106). Our culture limits us from seeing everything, but our culture allows us to see things others may not see. The church, through its missionaries and churches planted on the mission field, provides a platform for Christians of different cultures to come together and learn from each other. As members of a body we are limited, but in unity as a body, we see more clearly. Wisdom about God is found, in part, through intercultural relationships. As the theory of general revelation explains, other people can reveal things about God.

Discussion. Each of us has a personality with strengths and weaknesses, much like different cultures have strengths and weaknesses. What does your personality allow you to see about God that other personalities might not see? What does your personality limit you from seeing?

Based on the understanding that wisdom is found in relatedness, we can appreciate that cultures are gifts to the church. Missions connects cultures to each other and provides the global family a way to learn new things about God.

The theologian Amos Yong adds texture to the idea of revelations from God when he explains that God's revelation is transformational because it is found in relatedness. God's wisdom shared with Christians is not impersonal information. It is not like reading a manual that gives directions without calling us by name. Yong explains that because of the Holy Spirit, there is a living relational connection between God and the believer in Christ. God puts us in relationships that use our name and lovingly guide us. The Spirit is living and active, guiding the believer in the ways of Christ. The Spirit living in the heart of the believer is as real a relationship as any relationship. The Holy Spirit invites the church as a community in fellowship with God and each other to be part of a new world of new possibilities (Yong 2005, 298). The Holy Spirit uses the church to be a global family where we have names and unique identities, and we learn from each other.

I Corinthians 1 talks about wisdom and where it is found. It is found in relationships. Wisdom is found in knowing Jesus Christ. Jesus opens our minds to see what the world cannot see and what the world may even call foolish. Paul then adds this important insight in the letter to the Ephesians, "So that through the church the manifold wisdom of God might be made known to the rulers and authorities in the heavenly places" (Ephesians 3: 10 ESV). This means that the church is God's messenger in both heaven and on earth. The church reveals God's wisdom through words and relationships. The Word of God came through Christ, and Christ through the Holy Spirit empowers the church to reveal God's Word. The church proclaims the Bible and presents the sacraments. Both sacraments are based on relational connections, baptism is acceptance into God's family and Communion is a seat at the Lord's Table. The church, through relational missions, learns more about God as different cultures share their perspectives after coming to Christ. The church, through missions and connecting with other cultures becomes a storehouse of wisdom. Missions produces a church that has greater wisdom than it would have if the church remained in cultural isolation.

Discussion. What are the messages you can think of that are found in the Lord's Supper and in Baptism?

Looking Ahead: In the next lesson, we will explore how missions impacts the sending church and the larger global Christian Church. Missions is sacrificial for the sending church, but the sacrifice produces new life and energy in the sending church.

Reflection: How do you gain wisdom? Is it through what you experience or by what you hear from others? If you were to shift how you gain wisdom to "who you know" – what would that look like? To better understand this idea think of the difference between learning a skill as an apprentice, as opposed to being in a classroom. As you think about missions and missionaries, consider what they should be doing on the mission field that introduces people to wisdom. Read Paul's remarks about his missionary efforts in I Corinthians 2 in light of these questions.

Day Eight: Missions, the Road to Your Church's Renewal

Introduction: Missions is a two-way street of rebirth. The missionary goes, and those on the mission field are reborn by the gospel. At the same time, the sending church and its missionaries are also reborn in the process. This lesson will show why missions is crucial to church revitalization. If you want to see your church reborn and renewed, this lesson explains how missions can do that.

Scripture Review: Acts 10: 1-48

Acts 10 is a lengthy Bible story about missions that has several important themes. The story revealed Peter coming to a significant change in perspective, which was that God loves Romans. It revealed the Holy Spirit could come into the hearts of Gentiles, just as the Holy Spirit had come into Jewish hearts. And above all, the Acts 10 encounter changed the church leaders' understanding of what the Church of Christ was to be – it was to be a multicultural church. These revelations do not seem that significant 2,000 years later, but on that day, they were earth-shaking revelations.

Acts 10: 1-8, introduces us to the Roman captain Cornelius. He was a religious man and prayed each day. He was generous and gave to the poor. As a result (see verse 3), God sent an angel to Cornelius and told him that God had heard his prayers and seen his generosity. The angel (or the vision) told Cornelius to send two of his servants and one of his soldiers to Joppa to find a man named Simon (Peter).

Discussion. Why did the angel tell Cornelius to go find Peter and not just tell Cornelius the gospel message?

Acts 10: 9-16 presents a parallel story in which Peter has a vision. Peter's vision was the famous vision of a sheet being lowered with a variety of animals. There were all kinds of animals on display; some were inappropriate for a Jewish person to eat. Peter received a command, "kill and eat." Peter responded, "By no means." Then Peter reminded God that he was a Jew and devoted to God and Jewish dietary laws. God responded, "What God has called clean, do not call common" (ESV). This vision, probably because it was so upsetting, happened to Peter three times.

Acts 10: 17-23, Peter was confused and then there was a knock at the door. It was Cornelius' messengers. Peter met with them and learned a Roman Gentile wanted to talk to Peter about his visions. The messengers made it clear that Cornelius was not to be feared; he was a friend of the Jews.

Acts 10: 24-33, Peter arrived at Cornelius' home and found a crowd awaiting him. Cornelius, a Roman officer, showed profound respect for Peter. Peter noted the irony of the meeting, and he explained that it was un-Jewish for Jews to be in the home of a Gentile. However, explained Peter, he had a vision, and that is why he came. Cornelius then shared his vision with Peter. He explained he was told to find Peter in Joppa. Cornelius then announced to Peter, tell us what we need to hear from God.

Acts 10: 34-43, Peter shared ideas he probably had never preached before this meeting. His message reflected a total shift in perspective. Peter said that the gospel is for every nation. This concept of Gentiles joining the church was why Peter struggled with the vision about the diversity of animals. Peter then explained the significance of Jesus Christ. Peter did not try to win Cornelius' household to Judaism, but to Jesus Christ. Peter clearly explained the death and resurrection of Christ. He challenged all present to proclaim Christ.

Discussion. What do you think about this story and how God used visions to speak to those who did not know Christ? Why were prayers and generosity not enough for salvation?

Acts 10: 44-48, this account contains a moment of confirmation; the Holy Spirit was poured out in ways that all present experienced God. In this account, we learn that Peter came with Jewish friends; they too were amazed at what they saw. Cornelius' house was professing Christ, speaking in tongues, and worshiping God. Peter then decided the appropriate response was to baptize the entire household. The new believers were baptized in the name of Jesus Christ.

This story reveals something profound. Peter was changed as much as Cornelius. They both had visions, and they both came to new understandings about God. As the missionary Leslie Newbigin explains, the church was changed as a result of the conversion of Cornelius. The early church leaders reframed their understanding of evangelism and the church because of what Peter experienced in Cornelius' house. Thus, Newbigin concludes, the church is also converted when it does missions (Newbigin 1995, loc. 2474-2477).

Discussion. Explain what you think was Peter's conversion experience in the home of Cornelius. What do you think convinced Peter and made him a believer?

Mission Concept: Because of missions, the church is able to transcend its limited perspectives and be renewed (reborn).

In a real sense, we are all trapped by our culture, personality, and life experiences. Empathy is one way a person can see past these limitations. It is the ability to transcend our limited understanding by relating to others and seeing things as they see them (Bennett 2013, 49). The gospel and its ability to connect us to God and each other allows us to see and understand things about ourselves and others that in isolation, we do not see. For this approach to work, we need empathy.

As an example, let us contrast cultural individualism and collectivism. In a culture that promotes individualism, it is common in that culture to proclaim everyone is equal. The individualist culture expresses equality by not using honorary titles, avoiding strong outspoken leaders in favor of group collaboration, and having rules that impede favoritism. Fairness, which is treating each other as equals, is a virtue in individualistic cultures. The consequence is that the rule of law diminishes relationships and prioritizes right and wrong. Relationships are secondary to one's views, beliefs, and actions. Rules create equality, but they also depersonalize the community. Equality means it does not matter who you know.

In contrast, the communal culture sees loyalty to relationships as a virtue. Rules can be bent to accommodate relationships. Relationships are more important than rules. In the communal culture, favoritism can be a virtue; taking care of those we love is noble. Even if this means we promote our family and friends into good employment positions over more qualified people. Honorary titles and loyalty to an older family member (or person we honor) are ways a communal culture shows respect to others – respect is a virtue.

In both cases, these cultures have strengths and shortcomings. One stresses fairness as a virtue, and in contrast, the other stresses loyalty as a virtue. The only way to truly understand the other culture is through empathy. Empathy involves a deep relation connection with those of another culture by which one can see the world as the other person sees their world.

Discussion. Studies show that US Anglo Americans and Anglo Australians are among the most individualistic cultures in the world. Most Asian and Latino cultures are communal cultures. Based on your experiences, can you identify some of the shortcomings you see in individualistic cultures? And what are some of the shortcomings you see in communal cultures?

Milton Bennet notes that intercultural relationships take enormous energy. Trying to understand other people and cultures from our limited perspective is hard work (2013, 196). We, as Christians, in multicultural relationships must look around our blinders. The multicultural relationships that are part of missions force a new perspective. The mission professor Sherwood Lingenfelter explains that to transcend our culture, we need a multicultural community. His point is the intercultural community provides human interaction and accountability (2018, 74), thus transforming all in the community. In other words, the stress of understanding each other is worth the effort. The mission professor

Darrel Guder notes that the international interaction informs and transforms the sending church as much as the receiving church (2000, 201). The secular anthropologist Edward Hall puts it this way, "Years of study have convinced me that the ultimate purpose of the study of culture is not so much understanding of foreign cultures as much as the light that study sheds on our own culture" (Bennett 2013, 173). This dynamic of intercultural contact and renewal is seen in the interaction between Peter and Cornelius. Peter saw past his Jewish blinders. Cornelius saw past his polytheistic (many gods) cultural blinders. They were both transformed.

Discussion. As a Christian, what are some of your culture's activities or attitudes that you have set-aside because of your faith in *Christ?*

THINK

Mark Noll, a theologian and student of American Civil War theology, makes some interesting observations about US American Christianity in the 1800s. He explains that US Americans were very individualistic, and this cultural dynamic was reflected in their churches. The US American church believed most anyone could interpret scripture. In part, this explained why the Christian church in the USA was divided into so many denominations. Individualism also explained how US American Christians could justify things like slavery and war. Each geographic region had its own understandings of the Bible. Southerners and Northerners, in cultural isolation, were reflecting their culture and not God's Kingdom. Noll contends that the American Civil War was a failure of both the church and the US American Anglo culture. Southern Christians, by in large, used the Bible to justify slavery. And both Southern and Northern Christians used the Bible to justify war. The war drums were beating, initially, for economic reasons (2006, loc 2092). *Noll then observes that the church outside the USA, the non-American church, was baffled how the Southern USA church justified slavery and why both the North and South justified war. Noll contends that US American Christians simply reflected the views of the culture in their particular geographic area* (2006, loc. 1236). *Thus, how one interpreted Scripture depended on where they lived* (2006, loc. 1526).

How does geographic isolation diminish the church's ability to change and be renewed?

The German mission professor Henning Wrogemann explains there are two aspects to removing our blinders to see God's reality. One, the church provides the platform for the relational connecting needed for transformation. And two, the church must be culturally diverse (2016, 325). The church, through missions, connects different cultures, and the relational connection produces new awareness. Our relationships act as a mirror of our self thus guiding us to change. We see ourselves and others, and we see God's reality. The church is changed through missions; it is reborn. Richard Gaillardetz, a US American theologian, affirms a similar view, "The church is constantly being reborn in a rich global network of intercultural exchanges" (2008, 73). Missions is intercultural connecting, and vital to the church's rebirth. Missions moves the church from being a stagnant institution to a dynamic visionary movement that renews the entire church.

Action. Lookup online information about the Second Great Awakening. Read about this time in American history and note the diversity of people, the frequency of travel, and the different geographic areas where this event took place.

THINK

The father of the church growth movement, Donald McGavarn, credited his years on the India mission field as his source for understanding why churches grow. McGavarn's church growth movement swept the world in the 1980s. Many church leaders studied McGavarn's ideas, and new departments of Church Growth were opened in seminaries and denominations. What McGavarn learned in India impacted the entire Christian world. In fact, it was missions and the India mission field that brought revelations about church growth and rebirth to churches all over the world (Miles 1981, 13). It could be said that the India mission field brought a rebirth to the Christian church all over the world.

When speaking of church renewal, a key factor is leadership. Someone must lead the renewal. As explained above, missions provides the path, that is, new revelations about God's Kingdom that can be transformative. But those revelations need to be implemented; that is where leadership becomes vital. In the book, *To Change the Word*, James Hunter explains that change always comes from leadership. Change comes from the top down. His theory is that leaders must use their influence and connections to mobilize the masses. Change is not a grassroots movement, although the grassroots is moved. As Hunter explains, the grassroots need a leader to inspire and guide them to action. Change comes from an influential leader that provides the creative direction and manages the network of people following the new vision (Hunter 41-42). Cornelius was a Roman military officer; he had influence and connections. And Peter was a primary leader in the early church – scripture indicates he was often the voice of the Christian movement (Acts 2). These two men used their leadership positions and influence to change the church. The church was reborn, changing from a Jewish sect (Jews following Jesus) to a global movement (who-so-ever-will may follow Jesus). The church's rebirth was the result of an intercultural relationship between two men that experienced empathy. These leaders were able to profess to other people that respected and trusted them what their relationship had shown them about God.

Action. Think about leaders that you have had in your local church. What was their style of leading and why did people follow them? Think about yourself as a leader, what qualities do you have that you think people would be willing to follow? If you were to promote missions as a priority in your church, how would you do that?

Reflection: Church renewal is needed by all churches and comes from different experiences. One way to experience renewal is through intercultural relationships and worship. Think about the intercultural interactions you have had, maybe you have participated in a worship service of a different culture. What was your experience like? Was it inspirational? What are some ways you (and your church) can experience intercultural interactions? How can these interactions be done in such a way that they are a source of church renewal?

Bibliography

If you are interested in a more in-depth study of missions,
these are the books and articles cited in the Bible study:

Augustine. 2014. *On the Trinity*. Kindle edition. Aeterna Press.

Barth, Karl, and Keith L Johnson. 2019. *The Essential Karl Barth: A Reader and Commentary*. Kindle edition. Grand Rapids, Mich.: Baker Academic.

Boff, Leonardo. 2000. *Holy Trinity, Perfect Community*. Translated by Phillip Berryman. Reprint edition. Maryknoll, N.Y.: Orbis Books.

Bosch, David Jacobus. 2011. *Transforming Mission: Paradigm Shifts in Theology of Mission*. Twentieth anniversary ed, Kindle edition. American Society of Missiology Series, no. 16. Maryknoll, N.Y: Orbis Books.

Dodds, Adam. 2017. *The Mission of The Triune God: Trinitarian Missiology in The Tradition of Lesslie Newbigin*. Kindle edition. Eugene, Oregon: Pickwick Publications.

Gaillardetz, Richard R. 2008. *Ecclesiology for a Global Church: A People Called and Sent*. Theology in Global Perspective. Maryknoll, N.Y.: Orbis Books.

Green, Emma. 2019. "The Crisis of American Christianity, Viewed From Great Britain." *The Atlantic*, December 2019. https://www.theatlantic.com/politics/archive/2019/12/nt-wright-american-evangelicals-and-trump/602749/.

Guder, Darrell L. 2000. *The Continuing Conversion of the Church*. Seventh Impression edition. Grand Rapids, Mich: Eerdmans.

Harper, Brad, and Paul Louis Metzger. 2009. *Exploring Ecclesiology: An Evangelical and Ecumenical Introduction*. Grand Rapids, Mich.: Brazos Press, Kindle edition.

Hesselgrave, David J., and Edward Rommen. 2000. *Contextualization: Meanings, Methods, and Models*. Pasadena, Calif: William Carey Library.

Hiebert, Paul G. 1987. "Critical Contextualization." *International Bulletin of Missionary Research* 11 (3): 104–12.

Johnson, Darrell W. 2002. *Experiencing the Trinity*. Kindle Edition. Vancouver: Regent College Pub.

Kim, Van Nam. 2014. *Multicultural Theology and New Evangelization*. Lanham, Maryland: University Press of America, Inc.

Lewis, Gordon R., and Bruce A. Demarest. 1996. *Integrative Theology*. 3 vols. Grand Rapids, Mich: Zondervan.

Lingenfelter, Sherwood G. 2018. *Leadership In The Way of The Cross: Forging Ministry From The Crucible of Crisis*. Eugene, Oregon: Cascade Books.

Miles, Delos. 1981. *Church Growth, a Mighty River*. Nashville, Tenn: Broadman Press.

Moreau, A. Scott, Susan Greener, and Evvy Hay Campbell. 2014. *Effective Intercultural Communication (Encountering Mission): A Christian Perspective*. Kindle edition. Grand Rapids, Mich.: Baker Academic.

Newbigin, Lesslie. 1989. *The Gospel in Pluralistic Society*. Grand Rapids, Mich: Eerdmans.

———. 1995. *The Open Secret: An Introduction to the Theology of Mission*. Rev. ed, Kindle edition. Grand Rapids, Mich: W.B. Eerdmans.

Newbigin, Lesslie, and Paul Weston. 2006. *Lesslie Newbigin: Missionary Theologian: A Reader*. First Edition, First Printing edition, Kindle edition. Grand Rapids, Mich: William B. Eerdmans Publishing Company.

Noll, Mark A. 2006. *The Civil War as a Theological Crisis*. Kindle edition. The Steven and Janice Brose Lectures in the Civil War Era. Chapel Hill: University of North Carolina Press.

Ott, Craig, and Harold A Netland. 2006. *Globalizing Theology: Belief and Practice in an Era of World Christianity*. Grand Rapids, Mich.: Baker Academic.

Ott, Craig, Stephen J Strauss, and Timothy C Tennent. 2010. *Encountering Theology of Mission: Biblical Foundations, Historical Developments, and Contemporary Issues*. Grand Rapids, Mich.: Baker Academic.

Paas, Stefan. 2016. *Church Planting in the Secular West: Learning from the European Experience*. The Gospel and Our Culture Series. Grand Rapids, Michigan: William B. Eerdmans Publishing Company.

Pierson, Paul. 2009. *The Dynamics of Christian Mission, History Through a Missiological Perspective*. Kindle edition. Pasadena, Calif.: William Carey Library.

Piper, John. 2010. *Let the Nations Be Glad! The Supremacy of God in Missions*. 3rd ed. Grand Rapids, Mich: Baker Academic.

Pocock, Michael, Gailyn Van Rheenen, and Douglas McConnell. 2005. *The Changing Face of World Missions: Engaging Contemporary Issues and Trends.* Grand Rapids: Baker Pub. Group, Kindle Edition.

Richardson, Don. 2005. *Peace Child*. 4th ed. Ventura, Calif: Regal Books.

Walls, Andrew. 2006. *The Missionary Movement in Christian History: Studies in the Transmission of Faith*. Rev. Maryknoll, New York: Orbis.

Winter, Ralph D., Steven C. Hawthorne, Darrell R. Dorr, D. Bruce Graham, and Bruce A. Koch, eds. 2009. *Perspectives on the World Christian Movement: A Reader*. 4th ed. Pasadena, Calif: William Carey Library.

Wrogemann, Henning. 2016. *Intercultural Theology: Intercultural Hermeneutics*. Translated by Karl E. Böhmer. Kindle edition. Downers Grove: IVP Academic.

Yong, Amos. 2005. *The Spirit Poured Out on All Flesh: Pentecostalism and the Possibility of Global Theology*. Grand Rapids, Mich.: Baker Academic.

———. 2010. *In the Days of Caesar: Pentecostalism and Political Theology*. Grand Rapids, Mich: Eerdmans.

www.ingramcontent.com/pod-product-compliance
Lightning Source LLC
La Vergne TN
LVHW080329110826
845155LV00026B/228
9781945929311